The Gossamer Nature
of Random Things

The Gossamer Nature of Random Things

A First Collection of Poems

HOWARD BROWN

iUniverse, Inc.
Bloomington

The Gossamer Nature of Random Things
A First Collection of Poems

iUniverse books may be ordered through booksellers or by contacting:

iUniverse
1663 Liberty Drive
Bloomington, IN 47403
www.iuniverse.com
1-800-Authors (1-800-288-4677)

ISBN: 978-1-4759-5217-9 (sc)
ISBN: 978-1-4759-5219-3 (hc)
ISBN: 978-1-4759-5218-6 (ebk)

Library of Congress Control Number: 2012918473

Printed in the United States of America

iUniverse rev. date:10/15/2012

Contents

Rainy Day on the Mountain   1

Alicia's Backyard   2

Wolf River   3

Winter Sunday   5

Driving Up the Mountain   6

Walking to the Post Office   7

View from the Foot of the Grove   8

Rogue River   10

On the Porch   11

Early Morning, Lookout Mountain   13

Pebble Creek   14

Dog Days   15

Christmas Day   17

Kaleidoscope   18

Better Days   21

The Scars She Bore   22

Standing in Line   23

The Enigma of Friendship   24

On Being a Gulley   25

Her Number   27

Her Heart Could Not Be Still   29

Beware   30

Twilight   35

Gibbous Moon   36

Just Before Daybreak   37

Crescent Moon   38

Autumn Moon   39

The Moon and I   40

Wind Dream   45

The Beast 46

Dreamscape II 47

Motel Room 49

Message 50

Samsara 52

The Gossamer Nature of Random Things 57

Two Voices 58

Dreamscape I 59

Fait Accompli 60

Requiem 61

Loneliness and Solitude 62

Satori 63

Words Fail 64

Would You Know His Name 65

What If . . . ? 66

Ghost 68

Dedicated to my wife, Ann,
who always knew
the long sweep of time
would prove that you can, in fact,
make a silk purse out of
a sow's ear.

A FOREWORD TO
THE GOSSAMER NATURE
OF RANDOM THINGS

From poets, we receive our supply of epiphanies. For that reason poets are more important than lawyers and more necessary than plumbers, philosophers, stockbrokers, electricians and gastroenterologists. Because poets—and possibly physicists—constitute a kind of conduit of clarity that shows us the point of it all during our short appearance in what would be an otherwise *existable* . . . but fairly meaningless world. Poets can see the absolute, without any special equipment.

It is the poet who tells us the truth. And Howard Brown does exactly that. Howard provides the lines which complete the circuit—that fire in golden wire that carries the current that sends us the message we always want . . . one, perhaps, he's about to get when his cell phone blinks in "Rainy Day on the Mountain":

> *A message*
> *from beyond this place*
> *of rain and fog,*
> *of talking crows,*
> *aging dogs*
> *and Delphic cats.*

On another page, because life is composed mostly of small pieces that lie in the corners of moments, he writes to us about the beginning of a cross-country run through the woods along the Wolf River near Memphis. The words are simple, beautiful and true:

And in that moment of solitude, dream—

Of the whisper of bird wing on air,
the almost imperceptible scrape of scale and claw on sand
as the runners quit their places beneath the bridge
and, one by one, slip away into the forest.

Add that distillate to Howard's "Crescent Moon" in which, now at my eighth decade, I was comforted—and extremely delighted—by the flash of the following Damascene encounter:

. . . the magnificence of the waning moon
is undiminished.

Any reader who opens this beautiful book will be well served and fully rewarded. But throughout the whole selection, the lines every serious writer—who has ever toted hope in an overly stamped manila envelope containing his or her magnum opus, plus the *de rigueur* SASE—will love the most . . . are those four which, in "Walking to the Post Office," deliver Howard's solid, *andante* observation that:

There was a time
when Faulkner
walked up the street
to the post office too.

6/15/2012
Memphis, Tennessee

John Pritchard
Author of *Junior Ray* and *Yazoo Blues*

Place

*How hard it is to escape from places.
However carefully one goes they hold
you—you leave little bits of yourself
fluttering on the fences—like rags and
shreds of your very life.*

Katherine Mansfield

Rainy Day on the Mountain

Once again, the mountain is shrouded in fog.
Rain has fallen for days, an incessant downpour
which shows no sign of passing.

To the west,
a murder of crows waddle noisily
across the verdant expanse of the Commons.

Beneath the table,
the dog is curled at my feet,
drowsing contentedly in the midday gloom.

Across the room,
atop the worn back of an easy chair,
the cat has found his place of silent repose.

The red light on my cell phone winks—

A message
from beyond this place
of rain and fog,
of talking crows,
aging dogs,
and Delphic cats.

9/21/2009

Alicia's Backyard

Sitting placidly in my daughter's backyard,
a place of refuge,
where one can escape the wind
and bask in the failing warmth
of the October sun.

I close my eyes
and listen to the afternoon cries
of the children at play:
laughter one moment,
agony the next.

Simple things, to be sure,
but life is fleeting—
take your pleasure
where you find it.

10/4/2010

Wolf River

Listen to the silence,
the palpable absence of sound
which pervades the low ground along the river.

And in that moment of solitude, dream—

Of the whisper of bird wing on air,
the almost imperceptible scrape of scale and claw on sand
as the runners quit their places beneath the bridge
and, one by one, slip away into the forest.

Watch them move with a singleness of purpose
through a labyrinth, whose winding passages
are defined by sycamore, cypress, willow and gum.

Toward what do they move?

Perhaps to that secret place deep within the wood
where muscadines hang fragrant upon the vine,
and the sun filters down through the trees to spill golden
upon honeysuckle, jewel weed, sumac and fern.

Then, in a quickening moment, they have come and gone,
their passage marked only by a breach in the spider's web
and the frantic motes which dance in the luminous air.

In the distance, I hear them calling:
On, on, they cry, *on, on.*

And, as their voices fade and merge with the locusts' whir,
I realize that my question has been answered;
I need ask no more.

9/9/1988

Winter Sunday

Beyond the crystalline panes of the cathedral windows,
the leafless elms trace a tangled pattern
across a dark and lowering sky.

Wrapped in purple vestments, the priest stands before the altar
and recites a spiritual nostrum.

My attention drifts,
as he makes the sign of the cross,
a holy talisman to protect us from evil.

Then, as if waking from a dream,
I hear those about me softly chanting:

et ne nos inducas in tentationem, sed libera nos a malo.

And, as their voices float down the length of this holy place,
I murmur, sotto voce:

Save us not from the snares of Satan, Lord,
save us from ourselves.

2/14/2010

Driving Up the Mountain

Driving up the mountain,
the sun dappling the blacktop
where it breeches the forest canopy.

The air cool and brisk,
your mind
clear as a sounding bell.

Above it all,
a bone-white moon
perched high
in the midday sky.

10/10/2011

Walking to the Post Office

Walking up the street
to the post office.

The sky is blue,
the sun shining.

Manuscript in hand,
I try to think positive.

After all,
I tell myself,

There was a time
when Faulkner
walked up the street
to the post office too.

3/25/1991

View from the Foot of the Grove

High atop a granite pedestal
at the foot of the grove,
the Colonel stands
in stony silence.

Hand raised to shade his eyes
from the winter sun,
he peers to the east
down University Avenue.

In vain, he searches
for the comrades,
(long since gone to dust)
with whom he marched away.

Poised, vigilant, he waits;
waits for the bugles to sound,
the cannon to roar,
the vanquished to rise.

But what of the rest,
the nameless ones
for whom there was
no such noble cause,

Those for whom no monuments stand
as tangible reminders
that they have come and gone
and will come no more?

Who waits,
who remembers,
who heralds their passage?

9/26/1984

Rogue River

As the fog began to lift,
you could look down the flat, black surface of the river,
beyond the patina of evergreens
which cover the sides of the mountains,
to a point in the distance
where the opposing ridges tumble
to the bottom of the canyon.

And, at that precise juncture of granite and water,
a shaft of sunlight broke through the clouds,
transforming the air just above the river
into a sort of golden ether,

So that one might well imagine
that everything in life which had gone before
was leading, inexorably, to this precise moment,
and whatever else might follow
could not really matter.

10/24/2008

On the Porch

From your chair, look—

at the ferns
which fill the planters
on the edge of the porch,
how their fronds
move in the breeze;

the canopy
of the towering oaks
which stand
in the yard;

the couple
strolling lazily
up the street,
behind their panting dog.

Then listen—

to the discordant notes
of the tree frog;

the mournful coo
of a rock dove;

the moan of a train whistle
a mile to the south;

a car door slamming
somewhere down the block;

Look, listen,
absorb it all;
this is the marrow of life.

8/20/2008

Early Morning, Lookout Mountain

Floating toward daybreak,
fog envelops me
like a dream.

Time slows,
sound is muffled,
light distorted.

How can I put it—
like reality viewed
through a piece of gauze?

11/16/2010

Pebble Creek

Remembering the mottled carpet
of browning grass and grey-green sage
which cover the meadow floor;

the curving sweep of the stream
that parts its surface end to end;

the crumbling, volcanic slopes
of the mountains which rise beyond,
their ridges dark silhouettes on the horizon;

the endless expanse of cerulean sky,
broken only by a single column of towering cumulus;

you understand that these words
will never quite capture
the sacred nature of this untamed place.

9/3/2008

Dog Days

Now,
the dog days
of summer
are upon us.

The heat,
a demonic presence
dancing out of
a fevered dream;

the languorous air
so still, so passive,
its abiding torpor
almost visible;

the incessant
ringing of the cicadas,
a pervasive presence
which paints the backdrop

for the tenuous
sense of calm
which overlies
the breathless afternoon.

While far to the west,
clouds billow on the horizon,
their bellies purple
with a false promise of rain.

Such are the dog days
of summer,
such are the dog days
of the soul.

8/8/2008

Christimas Day

Snow has been falling
since before first light,
enormous, wet flakes
that dance in the wind
as they float to earth
from a pewter sky.

Beyond the window,
a smudge of scarlet
settles in the crepe myrtle,
positioning himself
for a pass at the feeders
which hang nearby.

And all the while,
I sit by the hearth,
listening to Stravinsky,
dreaming of spring.

12/25/2010

Kaleidoscope

Sheltered by a neon sky,
the mountain, a collage
of red, green and gold,
the magic of the landscape
enhanced by its own
inherent transience.

11/10/2011

People

The world is a stage, but the play is badly cast.

Oscar Wilde

Better Days

Watching him
through the window of the car
on this cold December Sunday,
I remember better days.

Days when his eyes
had the spark of the sun
on moving water.

Days when his hands
would flutter before his face
as he spoke,
like a covey of rising quail.

But now
he is nothing more
than a tired old man,

Who stands beside
a clap-board house,
chopping kindling
in the drizzling rain.

2/5/1988

The Scars She Bore

Like most everyone else,
she'd seen her share
of hard times,

yet, somehow,
had always managed to survive,
outdistancing whatever adversity
happened to come her way.

And, amazingly,
the evidence of her battles
was nowhere to be seen
upon her face.

Beyond question,
she was still
a strikingly beautiful woman,
the pure essence of style and grace.

So, only the very few
she ever allowed
to get close enough
to glimpse what lay inside,

could begin to fathom
the tell-tale scars she bore
upon her heart.

6/4/2008

Standing in Line

It was like this:
I was standing
in the checkout line
at the library.

The wait was really long
and as I stood there
looking at all the people
behind me,

I kept wondering
how so many geeks
could congregate in one place
at the same time.

Then I saw
this really flakey-looking guy,
back toward the end of the line,
staring in my direction,

And I began to wonder
exactly what conclusions
he might have reached
about me.

1/23/1988

The Enigma of Friendship

Like love, friendship is,
in the end,
a matter of the heart.

No expectations, no demands,
beyond a knowing smile
and a willingness, not only to listen,
but always to understand.

Springing from nothing,
moving toward nothing,
it is, simply, what it is,
nothing more, nothing less.

Yet only those for whom
it is a reality can actually
define it, can truly say,
we know.

2/11/2004

On Being a Gulley

There were worse things than being a Gulley.

You could have been a Turpin,
living out your life in ignorance and poverty
in a two-room shack on the edge of town,
cutting a little pulp wood now and then,
but never earning more in a week
than you could blow in a single Saturday night
drinking cheap whiskey and eating fried fish
in some piney woods juke-joint.

Or you could have been a Tull,
living likewise in ignorance and poverty
but lacking the mental acuity
to understand the essence of either;
too slovenly to work
and too much an outcast
to eat fish or drink whiskey
with anyone outside your own kin,
even if you had the money to do so.

Yes, there were worse things
than being a Gulley,
but being a Gulley was bad enough,
for, in all likelihood,
though you would have been
neither ignorant nor poor
and could pretty much
move in society as you pleased,
to us you would still have been white trash
just the same.

4/8/1988

Her Number

To have someone's number
was a casual expression,
something you heard
from time to time
but simply as metaphor,
a clever way of saying
you had a fix on someone.

Never once had he
considered the possibility
that each person
might actually have
a specific number
that was more or less
unique to them,

Until one day
he found himself
writing the figure,
eight million, one hundred
fifty-one thousand,
nine hundred forty-four,
across a sheet of paper.

And then,
as he stared blankly
at what he'd written,
he understood
that not only
does each person
have a number,
but this one was hers.

7/18/2008

Her Heart Could
Not Be Still

Like a tiny bird
flitting about
in the privet hedge,
her heart could not be still.

Each time she landed,
we wondered
if this was the place
she'd finally choose to stay.

But, inevitably,
a moment would come
when she'd sound
a single, tremulous note—
which was goodbye—
and then she'd fly away.

11/06/2002

Beware

Beware:

Of a man
who carries an overstuffed wallet
in the hip pocket
of double-knit trousers;

A jogger
wearing calf-length tube socks
and listening
to a transistor radio;

A woman
with a painted face
who smiles and tells you to
have a good one;

A slim-hipped blade
in puce
who only wants to know
the way to the park;

A preacher
who holds a Bible in one hand
and a collection plate
in the other;

A man
who dines
in public
with his cap on;

A postal worker
who claims
he's been
discriminated against;

Anyone
who has
never
smoked;

A man
who has
never tried
to grow a mustache;

A person
whose signature
you cannot
decipher;

Anyone
who says
they have the answer
to it all.

Beware!

5/2/1988

Lunar Reflections

*There are nights when the wolves
are silent and only the moon howls.*

George Carlin

Twilight

Beyond the dark silhouette of the hemlock,
a crescent moon appears,

a sliver of luminosity
in the fading afternoon light,

while I sit on the porch in silence,
as hummingbirds stir the air.

8/13/2010

Gibbous Moon

For a fleeting moment,
a waning, gibbous moon
shows its iridescent oval face
thru the veil of clouds
which mask the autumn sky,
then fades and disappears
once more in darkness.

9/19/2008

Just Before Daybreak

High above,
a pale moon
shows half its face,

the remainder
of its visage
shrouded deep
in shadow.

Beyond,
a scattering of stars
wink against
an infinity of darkness.

A darkness that
embraces you
like a broken dream,
as you await
the moment

when the sun
will finally creep
over the horizon
and begin to devour
the night.

9/22/2008

Crescent Moon

Though reduced to a fragile crescent
perched just above the dark horizon
in the eastern sky,
the magnificence of the waning moon
is undiminished.

Remembering,
the eye follows its curving edge,
then conjures the invisible remainder
of its full circumference.

Is this how it will be for us, as well,
our lives waxing and waning,
until we are finally reduced to a pale presence
slowly devolving to an imaginary line
in the mind of God?

9/27/2008

Autumn Moon

When darkness fell
at the end of each day,
we would stand
in the chill night air
and watch as the moon
showed its pale and pitted face
above the black rim
of the mountains.

A razor-thin crescent
that first evening,
then over a fortnight
each succeeding phase
appearing in its appointed turn:
quarter, gibbous, full.

And even when the lunar cycle
had finally run its waning, obverse course
and the moon had disappeared once more,
perfect orbs of light
still pooled upon our eyes.

9/07/2009

The Moon and I

Jogging through
the early-morning streets,
my feet sound a measured tattoo
against the pavement.

As I turn the corner,
the wind caresses my face,
a drop of sweat
trickles down my side.

To the west, the moon
hangs low on the horizon,
a lambent sphere of gold
in an endless expanse of darkness.

My gaze drops as I start up a hill.
I strain against gravity,
but even more against
the slow creep of time.

When I top the rise,
I look up again,
but now the moon is gone,
hiding its face behind a cloud.

And the notion
comes to me
that the moon and I
have much in common.

For I too tend
to wax and wane,
to shine brightly,
then disappear behind a cloud.

And there is
a symmetry of sorts
in this seeming cycle
of intransigence.

For appearances
are not always reality.
Whether waxing, waning
or hiding behind a cloud,
the moon is seldom
what it appears to be—
and neither am I.

4/16/2003

Darkness

*In the middle of the road of my life
I awoke in a dark wood where the
true way was wholly lost.*

Dante Alighieri

Wind Dream

Breaking the whisper
of the wind dream,
the crows
wing in.

Hesitating, they circle,
their calls
a cacophony
of mocking laughter.

Dark intruders,
they wheel
through my consciousness
with reckless abandon,

then move on,
floating lazily away,
as if their destination
did not really matter.

And now,
in their wake—silence,
and a deep sense
of abiding wonder.

1/30/1988

The Beast

Down the dark corridors
of our unremembered past
prowls the beast.

Jaw slack, his eyes
flickering orbs of fire,
he moves on cloven hooves
among the shadows.

Malevolent, caliginous,
he is the evil
which lurks within
the heart of man.

3/26/1984

Dreamscape II

An amorphous
cloud of birds
drifts across
the winter sky.

The morning is cold
and bleak,
but so is the dream
from the night before.

In the dream
a naked and bloodied man
runs pell-mell
across an open field,

his screams sounding
over an endless expanse
of plowed and muddy ground.

Why is he bleeding
and from what
does he flee?

Perhaps the dream is metaphor
for the grievous wounds
the dreamer bears
in his broken and weary life,

and the fact
that he cannot bring himself
to pause long enough
to allow his wounds to heal.

But just as his wonder is poised
to evolve to epiphany,
the bird-cloud dips to earth

obscuring both dream
and dreamer
within its boiling folds.

2/4/2008

Motel Room

This room
is a place
of vinyl sorrow,
the sad epiphany
of all the bad
which is yet
to come.

9/15/1988

Message

With a dull thump,
the bird collided
with the mirrored surface
of the window
behind my desk.

And the sound
had such a grim finality
about it, I almost
could not bring myself
to turn and look.

Of course, I did.
(Who can ever finally
put the small boy's
taste for the macabre
behind them?)

And there it sat
in the midst
of the neatly groomed
monkey grass,

wings spread,
head thrown back,
its beak opening
and closing,
again and again,

as if it had some
final message
to impart to me,
but knew in its heart
I would not listen.

2/04/2004

Samsara

You look at life
and ask yourself,
what, exactly, is the point of it all?

Because the most you can say
is that you'll spend
a given amount of time

working your way through
a seemingly endless
chain of days,

each link representing
a single period of twenty-four hours.
Each day invariably opening

with the promise that
it will actually
take you somewhere,

then simply looping back
and interlocking
with the link that preceded it.

Until, at last,
you reach that final link
only to find

that the end of the chain
is no different
from its beginning.

7/29/2008

Interior Monologue

All that we are arises with our thoughts. With our thoughts, we make the world.

The Buddha

The Gossamer Nature
of Random Things

Life, at best,
is a tenuous proposition,

a fortuitous convergence
of circumstance,

which hides behind
a façade of reasoned certainty.

And the glib trick
to living well,

lies in accepting
the gossamer nature of random things.

2/21/1988

Two Voices

A solitary cloud
floats across a vacant sky
and, suddenly, I am moved to tears.
Why? you ask, but I cannot say.

For the heart is an enigma,
keeping its own counsel,
parsing itself out
as it alone decides.

It's as if there were
two voices inside me:

one logical, calculating, rational to the bitter end;

the other impulsive, precipitous, eternally
thumbing its nose at the very notion of logic.

What a truly mystical thing then;
to see a cloud and weep,
and all the while another voice inside my head
tells me to save my sorrow
for something which really matters.

5/25/2004

Dreamscape I

Sliding through the darkness,
legs churning, torso bent low
over an improbable concatenation
of sprockets, gears, wheels and frame,
he moves in the night
like a line of quicksilver.

10/27/2003

Fait Accompli

Once you understand
that somewhere out there
in the existential jungle
a beast lies waiting,
and not simply waiting
for any hapless soul
who might wander by,
but for you in particular,

And you accept the fact
that there will be
no escape
from this final,
fatal encounter,
then life becomes
a simple proposition.

There's no longer
any need to worry,
because it's no longer
a question of the inevitability
of what will happen,
only how you'll choose
to face it.

10/15/2010

Requiem

Whatever else may be,
in time a day will come,
when, in a moment
of anguished epiphany,
tears well in your eyes
and stillborn words
roll from your tongue
like burning coals:

So, this was the
luminous eye
etched on the tapering
face of stone, the
silent archer whose
deadly arrow found
its mark, the birthright
traded for a bowl
of porridge.

But just as the
beckoning door
once stood open,
it will now have closed—
indeed, will have
vanished so completely
it might never have
been a door at all.

12/5/2009

Loneliness and Solitude

Tell me the difference
between loneliness and solitude.

One, thrust upon us
without regard for our desires.

The other, a matter
of reasoned choice.

Think of the bison
which stands alone in the meadow.

Picture the owl
calling softly from the heart of the wood.

Now, tell me the difference,
(if you can)
between loneliness and solitude

2/19/2011

Satori

With luck,
you finally reach
a point in life
where you understand
that most of the time
you've been allotted
is already gone.

And you begin to relax
and go with whatever
each remaining moment brings.

There's no longer
any good or evil, only truth.
And one of those improbable verities
is the inherent impermanence of it all;

the certain knowledge
that you can't hold on,
that despite your best efforts,
each succeeding moment
only brings you
that much closer to the end.

And with this knowledge
you finally grasp
the meaning of satori.

8/27/2008

Words Fail

In this uncertain life
there are things
for which
mere words
will not suffice.

Messages which
the eyes cannot read,
the ears do not hear,
and the tongue
cannot speak.

For they are
etched in braille
upon the heart.

7/03/2008

Would You Know His Name

If thoughts
were clouds,
could you
see the sky?

If life
was a dream,
would you choose
to wake?

If you met
the Buddha,
would you know
his name?

4/12/2006

What If . . . ?

What if
all the religions
and philosophies
and spiritual paths
man has dreamed up
since the beginning of time
are just so much bunk?

Intricate fairy tales
crafted to assure us
that life operates
on something
other than pure chance.

That death really is
the end of it all;
and when you croak
there's nothing else out there
but an infinity of nothing.

That God and the Devil,
heaven and hell,
angels and demons,
are just a figment
of someone's
fertile imagination.

Suppose that all there is,
is right here and now,
and whatever you want,
you'd better go ahead and grab,
because there won't be any
pie in the sky, bye and bye.

I mean, sure,
it's all a matter
of supposition,
but so is the opposite,
because no one ever proved it
one way or the other.

So, what if . . . ?

10/4/2005

Ghost

Sometimes what appears
to be an accident
turns out to be
no accident at all.

A favorite coffee mug
slipping from your hand,
shards of glass skittering
across the floor,
the quick red blood
washed down the kitchen sink.

A hard reminder
that the past really is
just that.

A convenient illusion,
another ghost you've needed
to say goodbye to
for a long, long time.

4/27/2012

AN AFTERWORD TO THE GOSSAMER NATURE OF RANDOM THINGS

Every genuine poet possesses a unique voice. It isn't crucial whether a poet is widely read or remains obscure, is prolific over decades or sparing in output: each perceives a private reality and from that wellhead of separateness is able to stitch words together in a masterful fashion, saying things no one else can say.

Howard Brown's poems mirror that uniqueness, netting moments suspended in time that others cannot capture and reflecting their flawless essence to us in language that conveys beauty, heartfelt appreciation, haunting emotion and, sometimes, loss. In our ever declining culture where the quality of words is no longer seriously regarded, there still are, and always will be, poets like Howard who can transport us with wonder and awe to that inner place where we intuitively belong so that we experience once again what is entirely natural as if it were a revelation.

6/11/2012
Lewiston, Idaho

R.J. Petrillo
Author of *Catching It Whole*